PRAISE FOR NINA SCHUYLER'S

Stunning Sentences:
A Creative Writing Journal

"Nina Schuyler's book is a creative antidote for anyone experiencing stuckedness, malaise, bad news, the doldrums. And just as useful for those who aren't feeling stuck but just want fresh, new ways to charge their writing. In her book you'll find a host of stunning sentences and prompts for she's a finder, she knows how to find the stunners, then shows you through specific examples how to bring forth your own great lines."

— Toni Mirosevich, author of *Spell Heaven*

. . .

"*Stunning Sentences* is simply wonderful. There are eighty magical prompts that author Nina Schuyler has carefully curated, providing writers a wide range of tips and techniques to try out. This workbook is a roadmap to hone skills and will give writers tools to effectively inject imagery and rhythm in their own work."

— Devi S. Laskar, author of *Circa* and *The Atlas of Reds and Blues*

How to Write Stunning Sentences

Stunning
SENTENCES

A Creative Writing Journal
with 80 Prompts from Beloved Writers
to Improve Your Writing Style

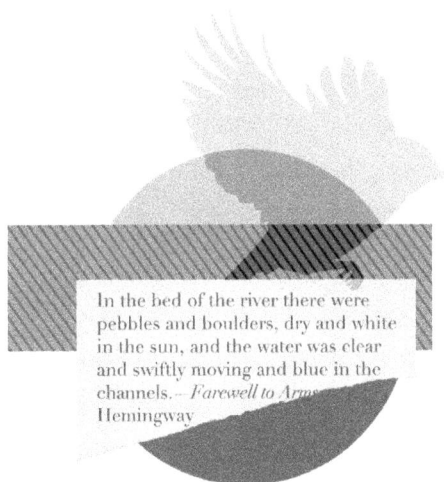

> In the bed of the river there were pebbles and boulders, dry and white in the sun, and the water was clear and swiftly moving and blue in the channels. —*Farewell to Arms*, Hemingway

NINA SCHUYLER

Sibylline
PRESS
AN IMPRINT OF ALL THINGS BOOK

To my students and those who love sentences.

Table of Contents

Introduction

I remember sitting in my phonology class, my eyelids flut-
tering with fatigue, watching the big hand on the industri-
al clock make its slow, syrupy movement. When will this
be over? Then I heard something that changed everything.

"What we're really doing is learning the music of language," said the professor.

Not often do I have epiphanies, but that was one of
those times. The class became infinitely more interesting.
I was learning the alphabet all over again, the sounds of
each letter, how they combine to vibrate my inner ear, my
mouth, my bones, my body. It held the same excitement of
learning to read. I was learning that the very sound of a
word contained meaning.

This was the beginning of my study of sentences,
though I'd always been drawn to them, their magical
spells reawakening the world. That class unlocked a door
to a room, and I'm still in that room, wandering around
making delightful, energy-infusing discoveries. The effect
of repetition, of changing the order of words, the emo-

tional effect of the right word, the right rhythm and sound. For me, a good story is inextricably linked to good writing, and good writing means style. Writers quickly learn every story has been told. But there's an opportunity to tell it differently through crafted sentences, to create a new musical composition.

There are so many ways to begin a story. A snippet of dialogue, an idea, an image, a character, either imagined or real, that grabs you by the neck and won't leave you alone. The entry to story can also be a stunning sentence.

This notebook is a place to play with sentences. You'll find more than sentences from published works that shine with elements of style—syntax, rhythm and sound, schemes and tropes, diction, and imagery. Maybe you'll find one of your favorite sentences here, but maybe you won't; I had to set a limit on how many mesmerizing sentences to include so you have room to write. I've taken the sentences apart, highlighting the style element and adding how I've used this sentence or what I love about it. The journal is organized by style technique, but many of the sentences include more than one technique, so the structure is somewhat fluid.

Maybe one of the sentences you write will be the origin of a new story for you.

Or not. This is a place to play around with language. Creativity needs play, playing around, disorder and randomness; it needs to unhinge from the strictures of logic and go a little wild.

It's also a place to revise. When I go through an early draft of a chapter or short story, I circle words and sentences that to my ear sound too flat, too one-note. The prompts might lead you to a better sentence to replace the one that thuds.

I've also included two glossaries. You are, most likely, a lover of words, which means you probably care deeply about how terms are defined. Let me say there are many ways to define these terms, and the explanations could have been much longer. These are simply my definitions, and they are compressed.

I'm excited to share with you this room full of delightful discoveries.

PART ONE

Syntax

"My only duty was to describe
reality as it had come to me—to
give the mundane its beautiful
due."—John U⁓⁓⁓

1

When I'm revising, I'll take a traditionally structured sentence and change the word order to see if it sounds better.

Very romantic, how we first met.

—*Grief is the Thing with Feathers*, Max Porter

You can draw attention to the sentence by using hyperbaton (also called anastrophe if only one word is switched), or the inversion of usual order of words. Start with a sentence written in the traditional way, subject/verb predicate. If Porter's sentence was written in the usual word order it would be, "How we first met was very romantic." Now move the ending to the beginning.

2

This sentence offers a subtler, quieter form of hyperbaton.

Around him sat four or five of the younger guides.

—*River in the Dark*, Jean Speiser

To emphasize the subject of your sentence invert the order by placing it at the end. It also creates a different rhythm. Using traditional syntax, the sentence would be: "Four or five of the younger guides sat around him." Write a traditional syntactical sentence. Now move the adverbial phrase to the beginning, followed by the verb, and end with the subject.

3

Through unusual syntax and a rupture in parallelism, voice is immediately established.

> *Here was himself, young, good-looking, snappy dresser, and making dough.*
>
> —*Sweet Thursday*, John Steinbeck

Instead of traditional syntax (He was ...), try something different to create a strong voice. Describe the subject (subject complement) with four adjectives, but disrupt the parallelism with the last descriptor—like "making dough."

STUNNING SENTENCES

4

I love this sentence because it smashes together two unexpected things and reveals how the character views the world. The thrill of language!

That was a terrible thing to ask of someone; also then I had to do my laundry on Thursdays.

—"Angel's Laundromat" by Lucia Berlin

This is a compound sentence with a semicolon connecting the two independent clauses. The first independent clause focuses on the emotional; after the semicolon, the second independent clause focuses on the practical. Try to connect two things that are not usually found together or are in some way different.

5

In this sentence, the syntax mimics the content, a technique called syntactic symbolism. We wind our way through the sentence through many prepositional phrases, just as the men and women have to navigate their way to the trains.

> *The procession of men and women from the street into the station and down the escalators towards the trains becomes a movement from a world above to an underworld of death.*
>
> —*The Lyrical Novel*, Ralph Freedman

Start with a right-branching sentence and elongate the subject through prepositions (from/into/down/towards). These prepositions create movement. Now can you end with antithesis (world above/underworld)?

6

Here's another one. We have to wade through the modifying phrases to find the bottle of Jim Beam.

> *In the car, in the space under the spare tire, hidden by a half-used roll of paper towels, is a fifth of Jim Beam.*
>
> —"All the Way in Flagstaff, Arizona" by Richard Bausch

To create suspense, write a left-branching sentence (the base clause at the end) with three modifying phrases or clauses. Now put the most important information at the end.

7

And another. This sentence feels like a path as we meander along, turning and going around and across.

> *The path runs straight as a plumb-line, worn smooth by feet and baked brick-hard by July, between the green rows of laidby cotton, to the cottonhouse in the center of the field, where it turns and circles the cottonhouse at four soft right angles and goes on across the field again, worn so by feet in fading precision.*
>
> —*As I Lay Dying*, William Faulkner

Write a right-branching sentence, with your subject/verb predicate at the beginning. Now add three modifying phrases that give more detail to the subject. Can you include alliteration (baked/brick/between), and polyptoton (cotton/cottonhouse)?

8

I love Salter's eloquent sparseness, which allows in so much light on the other side of language, making his sentences luminous.

> *He earned money, he was liked by his clients, he could draw beautifully.*
>
> —*Light Years,* James Salter

Write three independent clauses that describe a character. Now use asyndeton, which is the elimination of commas and results in comma splices to create speed. (Your English teacher would disapprove). Note here there is a sense of a round character because of the spectrum of details—from earning money to drawing.

9

Imperatives always jar me. They make me sit up and pay attention. The child in me has the urge to obey, almost as if my parents are perched on my shoulder, telling me what to do.

Bite your tongue. Close your mouth.

—*I'm from Nowhere,* Lindsay Lerman

Write at least two imperatives. The subject "you" is implied and ushers in intimacy with the reader.

_____

_____

_____

_____

_____

_____

_____

_____

_____

_____

10

By the end of this sentence, I really see her. How powerful the accumulation of details, how necessary.

> *I examined her face, the eyes so heavily mascaraed, but large and gray, the lines extending from her lips that the makeup failed to hide, the creases in her forehead.*
>
> —*The Claimant*, Hollis Alpert

This is a cumulative sentence; it accumulates or adds details as it goes on, all of which refers back to the opening independent clause, specifically the direct object—her face. There is a forward motion created by the new details and a spiraling motion as they send the reader to the base clause. Open with a subject and verb and direct object. Now modify the direct object (face) with at least three free-modifying phrases.

11

Even if the voice of a story isn't highly stylized, this sentence shows you can still create a little music.

The view was of cascading expensive houses, pruned and prim.

—"In the Event" by Meng Jin

This is a right-branching sentence. Use two adjectives to describe a noun and place those adjectives after the noun. Create more music by using alliteration.

_____

_____

_____

_____

_____

_____

_____

_____

12

I love cumulative sentences! You easily create rhythm and music, and because of the alliteration, I really feel the throbbing music.

Claudius Van Clyde and I stood on the edge of the dancing crowd, each of us already three bottles into one brand of miracle brew, blasted by the music throbbing from the speakers.

—"No More than a Bubble" by Jamel Brinkley

Use a right-branching sentence and open with an independent clause (the subject/verb predicate). The modifying information that follows refers back to the independent clause. Try playing with alliteration and thread it through the entire sentence. Here you have bottles/brand/brew/blasted. Then there's the consonance of "throbbing." The technique brings attention to the alliterated words.

13

Another cumulative sentence. With present participles (-ing words) you create a sense of an ongoing feeling. They also inject more energy into the sentence because even though they function as an adjective, they also have the flavor of their origin, which is a verb.

> *He played the entire width of the table, his body leaning and twisting as his fingers swept the keyboard, left hand pounding at those chords that jangled silverware, while his right hand raced through runs across tacky oilcloth.*
>
> —"Chopin in Winter" by Stuart Dybek

Write a right-branching sentence, with the subject and verb predicate at the beginning. Now add three or four modifying phrases that refer back to the subject ("he" in the above sentence), providing more specificity. Can you use -ing words, like Dybek did with leaning/twisting/pounding?

14

Interrogatories create urgency in story—why are the questions coming up now? There is a feeling of things being unsettled, unstable.

> *Thirty-one years old, healthy and whole, married to a fourth husband (why four?) who loved me, with a bodyguard of children (why so many?)— what was I frightened of?*
>
> —*The Pumpkin Eater*, Penelope Mortimer

Begin with factual details about your character. At the end, add an em dash and a question. Now go back and embed two more questions in the overall sentence using parentheticals.

STUNNING SENTENCES

15

In this sentence, the narrator is listening to music from another apartment. I love how the music becomes a tangible presence, permeating everything.

I kept catching wisps of it in the air shaft, behind the walls and ceilings, under bathwater.

—"Chopin in Winter" by Stuart Dybek

Open with your subject and verb; now include a direct object (here it is "it," which refers to music). Add three modifying phrases that make the direct object more specific. Can you create assonance—the repetition of vowel sounds (wisps/it) (shaft/bath) (walls/water)?

16

Left-branching sentences make me feel like I'm the lucky recipient of a storyteller who has mastered the temporal aspects of the narrative.

> *While the butler now hovered behind him with the coffee pot, Mad Mack's harsh voice rang out, deploring the fact that his shaving water had been tepid.*
>
> —*Fools of Fortune*, William Trevor

Open with a dependent clause by using a subordinate conjunction (while, after, though, even, even if …). Now write your independent clause (subject and verb predicate). One effect is suspense by delaying the independent clause.

17

Here's the great stylist Toni Morrison displaying her talents, invoking many fantastic style techniques in a single sentence.

> *Certain seeds it will not nurture, certain fruit it will not bear, and when the land kills of its own volition, we acquiesce and say the victim had no right to live.*

—*The Bluest Eye,* Toni Morrison

For two independent clauses, use hyperbaton—inversion of the usual order of words—to draw attention to the sentences. (With traditional syntax, the sentence would have been "It will not nurture certain seeds" and "It will not bear certain fruit."). Use anaphora for these two clauses, opening with the same word ("certain") to create a rhythm. And then epistrophe, the repetition of an ending clause or phrase ("it will not"). Use a conjunction and add a dependent clause ("and when"), which creates a build to your final independent clause. Want more style? Weave in assonance (it/will/kills/victim/live).

18

I know I'm in for a surprise when a sentence uses the conjunction "but" because it turns a sentence in a new direction.

I was once foolish enough to believe knowledge would clarify, but some things are so gauzed behind layers of syntax and semantics, behind days and hours, names forgotten, salvaged and shed, that simply knowing the wound exists does nothing to reveal it.

—*On Earth We're Briefly Gorgeous*, Ocean Vuong

Start with a right-branching sentence, then use the conjunction "but." Now use anaphora—beginning phrases or clauses with the same word ("behind"), and balance ("syntax and semantics," "days and hours") and series ("forgotten, salvaged and shed") for rhythm and sound. Can you add alliteration (some/syntax/semantics/salvaged/shed/simply)?

19

With a long sentence, you can create so much action—the kissing and turning and pushing.

> *Mitko turned to me and kissed me, deeply and searchingly and possessingly, at the same time pushing me backward down the hallway toward the bedroom, pushing me and perhaps also using me for support, to the broad bed where we had lain together earlier and where now we lay down again.*
>
> —*What Belongs to You*, Garth Greenwall

Write a right-branching sentence, with the subject and verb predicate at the beginning. Now use series (three things) and add three adverbs to describe your verb as Greenwell did with "deeply and searchingly and possessingly." Go ahead—create a new word like Greenwall did with "possessingly." Create a sense of simultaneity with the words "at the same time," or "as" and add another verb (pushing). Repeat that last verb and add a dependent clause (where …).

20

This left-branching sentence does so much work to establish the character, family dynamics, and his age.

> *At the age when I was always being warned by my mother not to get overheated, spring began on that evening when I was first allowed to go outside after dinner and play kick-the-can.*
>
> —"First Love and Other Sorrows" by Harold Brodkey

Open with modifying phrase and a dependent clause. This opening delays your base clause (spring began). Now add one more dependent clause (when I was...), which adds more details to the base clause.

21

Such suspense! This sentence makes me want to know what the narrator feels.

I feel—and the anxiety is still vivid to me—that I might easily have failed before I began.

—*Literary Occasions*, V.S. Naipaul

This is a mid-branching sentence that generates suspense. Usually, a mid-branching sentence is created by separating the subject and verb. Here, you're going to separate the transitive verb "feel" from the direct object (the direct object answers the question: feel what?). Delay the direct object by using an em dash to contain parenthetical information.

22

The syntax of this sentence simulates the water rising—which is so cool!

The water would rise inch by inch, covering the grass and shrubs, covering the trees and houses, covering the monuments and the mountain tops.

—*A Portrait of the Artist as a Young Man,* James Joyce

Open with a right-branching sentence. Now add modifiers, the first one short, then the next one longer in terms of syllables, and so on. Can you add anaphora, repeating the same words at the beginning of each modifying phrase ("covering")? Use balance, the pairing of two things, in your modifying phrases.

23

I always forget about mid-branching sentences, but this one reminds me of their powerful, suspenseful effect.

To look at them, these field instruments—these containers embedded and tucked and stashed about—seem benign and dumb and exquisitely unperturbed.

—"Shakers" by Daniel Orozco

To create a mid-branching sentence, separate the subject (instruments) from the verb (seem) with modifying information. In the modifying information that separates the subject and verb, can you write three modifiers (embedded, tucked, stashed)? After the verb, add three adjectives to describe the subject (benign/dumb/unperturbed).

Rhythm and Sound

"Sound is the abstract vitality
of our speech." —Robert Frost

24

I often forget about hyphenated adjectives. This sentence has so much bounce and fast-paced rhythm because of them.

> *So even though he wears button-up-the-front sweaters and round-toed shoes, he's a kid, a strapling, and candy could still make him smile.*

> —*Jazz,* Toni Morrison

Use a left-branching sentence, which opens with a dependent clause (So even though ...). In that dependent clause include two hyphenated adjectives to describe your direct objects. End your sentence with two base clauses. In Morrison's sentence, the first base clause is "he's a kid." The second one, "candy could still make him smile."

25

I had a professor who once told the class never to use adverbs. Groff's sentence reminds me not to blindly follow every bit of advice.

> *Love that had begun so powerfully in the body had spread luxuriantly into everything.*
>
> —*Fates and Furies*, Lauren Groff

Balance, the pairing of two things, creates music. Write a sentence that has two verbs and pair it with two adverbs, as Groff does with "powerfully" and "luxuriantly."

26

Oh, the rhythm of balance, the pairing of two things, and series, the realm of three things. Such beautiful music!

> *In the bed of the river there were pebbles and boulders,*
> *dry and white in the sun, and the water was clear and*
> *swiftly moving and blue in the channels.*
>
> —*Farewell to Arms*, Hemingway

Open with two prepositional phrases that establish place. Now comes your base clause. Use a linking verb (is/was) and follow with two nouns connected with "and." To describe those nouns further, use two adjectives and connect those with "and." Add a second base clause with another linking verb. Add three adjectives and use polysyndeton, the overuse of conjunctions to connect those.

27

Not a typo! Keep reading and you'll know why I capitalized some letters.

The TRUCKS THUMPED HEAVily PAST, ONE by ONE, with SLOW inEVitable MOVEment, as she STOOD INsigNIficantly TRAPPED between the JOLTing BLACK WAGons and the HEDGE.

—"Odour of Chrysanthemums" by D.H. Lawrence

The capitalization represents the heavier stresses in this sentence. A heavier stress is an emphasis on a syllable. Here, Lawrence clustered three hard stresses (trucks thumped heavily) to capture the heavy weight of the trucks and to slow down the sentence. He added even heavier stresses after that for the same reason. Write a sentence with three hard stresses. Make sure this is the point where you want the reader to slow down.

28

More practice with heavier and soft stresses.

Over the SCORCHED THROAT of the reACtor,
aBOVE but not-so-far beYOND the sarCOphagus
hiding the HOT HEART of CherNObyl, HOME
into the priMEeval OAKS of the forBIdden
ZONE, BLACK STORKS GLIDE, WHITE BElies
exPOSED, RED BEAKS FLASHing

—*Song & Silence*, Melanie Rae Thon

The three hard stresses, BLACK STORKS GLIDE, conveys
a sense not of lightness and flying and gliding, but struggle.
Which is the point: the birds have been exposed to radiation.
Compare it to a fluid, flowing sentence: the black storks
flew and swooped and swung low and high, round the trees
and little houses. Create a sentence with three hard stresses
for something that should be flowing but is not.

29

When I first read this sentence, I wrote it down. I knew I wanted to remember it, to try something like it.

> *My HEART WHAPPED in my THROAT and ALL*
> *I could THINK was HOW to KEEP them, HOW*
> *to KEEP them.*
>
> —*Euphoria*, Lily King

King uses hard and soft stresses to mimic a heartbeat. Can you play with hard and soft stresses to capture the rhythm of something?

30

There's a pattern to the rhythm in this sentence—can you hear it? It's called a cretic pattern, a hard stress, followed by a soft stress, followed by a hard stress.

> *She was fair and sharp in a green bikini, though it*
> *was May in Maine and cold.*
>
> —*Fates and Furies,* Lauren Groff

Write a right-branching sentence, with your subject and a linking verb at the beginning. Use balance and include two adjectives to describe your subject and use the cretic rhythm, "FAIR and SHARP." Can you do it again, like Groff did with "GREEN bi-KI-ni?" And again, "MAY in MAINE?"

31

Adjectives can create a slower rhythm. In this case, the technique mimics the light unable to spread.

> *Here at the end of the hall, through windows exteriorly screened against vandalism, light from outdoors entered the school and, unable to spread in the viscid, varnished atmosphere, remained captured, like water in oil, above the entrance.*
>
> —*The Centaur,* John Updike

Write a left-branching sentence to create suspense, postponing the base clause, which is "light from outdoors entered" in Updike's sentence. Use "and" and add more modifiers describing the subject. To slow down the sentence further, use two adjectives ("viscid, varnished"). Add another verb, continuing the base clause (here it's "remained"). Can you end with a simile?

32

Here's the way Hemingway writes his long sentences. There is a flow to it, a feeling that things are happening simultaneously.

> *She had wonderfully beautiful hair and I would lie sometimes and watch her twisting it up in the light that came in the open door and it shone even in the night as water shines sometimes just before it is really daylight.*
>
> —*Farewell to Arms*, Ernest Hemingway

Write three independent clauses. Now connect them with the conjunction "and" to create more rhythm and flow.

_____

_____

_____

_____

_____

33

Woolf is considered one of the most rhythmic prose writers. I never get tired of reading her writing. Never.

> *The car had gone, but it had left a slight ripple which flowed through glove shops and hat shops and tailors' shops on both sides of Bond Street.*
>
> —*Mrs. Dalloway,* Virginia Woolf

Write a right-branching sentence. Now add the coordinating conjunction "but" and add a second base clause. Can you use personification as Woolf does with the car leaving a slight ripple? Want more? Use epistrophe, repeating the last word in a phrase or clause ("shops") for rhythm and emphasis. Can you hear the patterns: GLOVE shops and HAT shops and TAIlor's shops? Use polysyndeton, the overuse of conjunctions to connect the nouns.

34

Can you hear the pattern of two softer stresses followed by heavier stress?

We were ALL there the DAY Mr. MAN came to TOWN, driving that BLISter-COLored TIN CAR.

—"Mbiu Dash" by Okwiri Odour

Write a simple sentence using this pattern of stresses, soft, soft, heavier. Then disrupt the pattern to emphasize the most important part. Here, the rhythm changes with Mr. MAN (heavier stresses capitalized).

35

In this sentence, the setting becomes so vivid and the rhythm makes us stand still, as the narrator is doing.

> *I was old enough to feel embarrassment at standing there alone with my mother, beside a wind-stunted spruce tree, on a long spine of shale.*

—"Flight" by John Updike

Write a right-branching sentence with your subject and verb predicate at the beginning. Now use modifying phrases to describe the setting, looking for opportunities to grow your sentence with adjectives. Here, Updike used adjectives to describe the tree and the shale. With the adjectives, can you create a rhythm so they echo each other? I'll show you what I mean. The hard stresses are in capital letters. WIND STUNTed SPRUCE TREE; LONG SPINE of SHALE.

36

The cluster of adjectives at the end of the sentence makes me stay right here, in one spot, listening to the strokes spaced and tranquil.

> *I stood in the belly of my shadow and listened to the strokes spaced and tranquil along the sunlight, among the thin, still little leaves.*
>
> —*The Sound and the Fury,* William Faulkner

Write a right-branching sentence with two verbs (stood/ listened). Can you add personification (belly of my shadow)? Now add alliteration (stood/shadow/strokes/spaced/ sunlight/still; and listened/little/leaves) and assonance with three adjectives (thin/still/little). Want more? Write a pattern of two consecutive hard stresses, STROKES SPACED/ THIN STILL to slow down the sentence.

STUNNING SENTENCES

37

I have children, and this sentence captures how, when they hit their teen years, time rushes by.

> *She is thirteen, she will be fourteen, fifteen, sixteen.*
> —*The Blue Flower,* Penelope Fitzgerald

This sentence uses asyndeton—the elimination of conjunctions—to create speed. If you were writing a grammatically correct sentence, you'd need the conjunction "and" or a semicolon between the two clauses, but you want quickness. Write two independent clauses and connect them with a comma (called a comma splice). Can the second sentence use a future tense verb (will)? Describe your subject with adjectives and don't use a conjunction for your final adjective.

STUNNING SENTENCES

38

Long sentences are like open doors for interesting rhythms.

> *I heard a chair groan as someone rose from it, and then a quieter, extended exchange I could make little of, though I knew it must mean they had something to discuss, and I realized, with a sharp clenching in the pit of my stomach, that I was surprised, that for all my anxiety I hadn't really believed I had it, and I thought of R., of what I would have to tell him and of how he would respond.*
>
> —*What Belongs to You*, Garth Greenwell

You can do this! Remember: often with a long sentence there is more than one base clause. A good way to analyze a sentence like this is to spot the base clauses. In this one, there are three: 1) "I heard a chair groan ... 2) "I realized ..." 3) "I thought of R.." Start with a right-branching sentence, opening with a base clause. Now add a dependent clause (though I knew ...). Add the second base clause followed by two relative clauses (that); finally use a conjunction and add a third independent clause ("I thought of R.").

39

I love how the proliferation of adjectives and noun slows down the sentence, capturing the sense that knowledge is consuming everything.

> *I understood that knowledge was a dwarfing, obliterating, all-consuming thing, and to have it was to both be grateful and suffer greatly.*
>
> —"The Resident" by Carmen Maria Machado

Write a right-branching sentence and include three adjectives ending in –ing and a noun, such as "thing," creating rhythm (dwarfing, obliterating, all-consuming). Now use a conjunction and add another independent clause that uses balance, the pairing of two things, and antithesis, or opposites, as Machado does with "grateful and suffer."

_____

_____

_____

_____

40

The physicality of the character is firmly on the page before he speaks. The hard stresses create a sense of heaviness and hardness.

> *With his thick back and small thighs, his head*
> *shaggy and aggressive and his hands folded small*
> *and timid on his belly, he spoke to Herzog in a*
> *diffident, almost meek tone.*
>
> —*Herzog,* Saul Bellow

This is a left-branching sentence, with modifying phrases and clauses at the beginning. Use balance—the pairing of two things: "thick back and small thighs," "shaggy and aggressive," "small and timid" in the phrases and clauses, delaying the base clause (here, it's "he spoke to Herzog ..." Can you create a pattern of two heavier stresses? THICK BACK/SMALL THIGHS.

41

With poetry, you have line breaks and stanzas. With prose, you have punctuation marks to create phrase groupings. Think of the syntactic phrase as the basic unit of analysis for prose rhythm. Now, here is Morrison creating a wonderful rhythm!

> *They wanted to see the joy in her face as they settled down to play checkers, knowing that even when she beat them, as she almost always did, somehow, in her presence, it was they who had won something.*
>
> —*Sula*, Toni Morrison

One way to build tension and suspense in a sentence is to include phrases or clauses, which delay the ending. Start with a right-branching sentence, add a dependent clause (as they settled …). Now add another dependent clause (even when she …) and include two or three short phrases or clauses to delay the final independent clause (it was they …).

42

When I want to get ready to write, when I want more rhythm in my writing, I pick up Virginia Woolf. When I want to write freshly, originally, I pick up Virginia Woolf.

> *She had a sense of being past everything, through everything, out of everything, as she helped the soup, as if there was an eddy—there—and one could be in it, or one could be out of it, and she was out of it.*
>
> —*To the Lighthouse,* Virginia Woolf

Use a right-branching sentence. Now use epistrophe—the repetition of a word, or words, at the end of clauses or phrases—to create rhythm and heightened emotion. Here she repeats three times "everything." Add two dependent clauses (as she, as if there) and finish by using epistrophe again, as Woolf does with "it."

PART THREE

Schemes and Tropes

3

When you choose an unusual
adjective, it should do more
work than adding description
because you're d~

43

Think of time as clay. Will you stretch it? Compress it? Here it is wadded tightly into one sentence.

> *He entered Rice University as a prospective double-E major and left it with a degree in French, having in the meantime managed KTRU, the campus station, for three semesters.*
>
> —*Strong Motion*, Jonathan Franzen

Write a right-branching sentence with your subject and verb predicate at the beginning. Use antithesis, or opposites and write two verbs in that opening sentence (entered/left) to create a big sweep of time. There's more antithesis with "double-E major" and "French." Use a modifying phrase or clause that adds more information to the base clause.

44

Rather than use abstractions, concreteness can make things far more interesting.

> *Aboveground monsters were everywhere, with terrible hair and red neckties.*
>
> —*The Hero of This Book*, Elizabeth McCracken

Metonymy, taking an attribute of the whole, is so powerful. Instead of naming the humans who are doing terrible things, McCracken takes an aspect of them, their monstrous actions, and calls them monsters, giving them specific details. Think of the whole of a type of person. Now think of attributes and use this as their name.

STUNNING SENTENCES

45

Imagine if this list was connected by coordinate conjunctions. It would be so much smoother. As it is written, it creates a feeling of being hit by sounds.

Car horns. Garbage trucks. Ferry whistles. The thrum of the subway.

—*Let the Great World Spin,* Colum McCann

Ellipsis, the omission of words, can speed up the story and create a jagged rather than smooth sensation. Make a list of nouns with adjectives, perhaps to convey the setting, as McCann did, and don't add verbs. Now separate the list of nouns with periods.

STUNNING SENTENCES

46

My high school English teacher is hissing in my ear about commas, but I've learned there are times to choose style over proper grammar.

They climb quickly into long johns and wool shirts and sweaters and parkas.

—"The Bridge" by Daniel Orozco

Polysyndeton is the overuse of a conjunction to create a rhythm, with the "and" always a soft stress. It also emphasizes every word in the list. Make a list of at least four words and use a coordinating conjunction (for, and, nor, but, or, yet, so) instead of commas.

47

Here's another one to upset my English teacher.

She was exasperation, she was torture.

— *Ada,* Vladimir Nabokov

Here you get to play with synecdoche—the part stands for the whole, or, less commonly the whole for the part. Synecdoche is very similar to metonymy. Write two sentences that equate the subject of your sentence to an emotion or action. To create speed, use asyndeton—eliminating the conjunction or semicolon between your two independent clauses, and, yes, creating a comma splice.

48

I love the repetition because it wonderfully heightens the emotion.

> *Dorcas is happy. Happier than she has been anytime.*
>
> <div align="right">—<i>Jazz,</i> Toni Morrison</div>

Try this technique called polyptoton, in which you repeat words with the same root but different forms or endings, as in "happy" and "happier."

49

How to build surprise? Set up a pattern, then depart from it.

> *The air was the blue of a pool when there are shadows, when the clouds cross the turquoise surface, when you suspect something contagious is leaking something camouflaged and disrupted.*
>
> —"Tall Tales from the Mekong Delta" by Kate Braverman

Use a right-branching sentence. Now use anaphora—repeat the same word three times ("when")—and write three modifying clauses adding more description. The anaphora provides cohesion, and yet the last clause departs from the earlier clauses. In the first two "when" clauses, we're in the natural world. The final clause deviates into what is probably the human-made world. In that final clause, can you use anaphora again and repeat a different word ("something")?

50

The art of compression!

Historically, he has always been a taker and a giver.
—"Something Street" by Carolyn Ferrell

Antithesis, or opposition, creates tension at the sentence level. Here, Ferrell uses "taker" and "giver." Describe your subject using antithesis.

51

I love personification, how the song in this sentence comes alive.

> *The songs caressed her, and while she tried to hold her mind on the wages of sin, her body trembled for redemption, salvation, a mysterious rebirth that would simply happen, with no effort on her part.*
>
> —*The Bluest Eye,* Toni Morrison

Do you have two aspects of someone at war? This is a good model to capture that. Use a right-branching sentence. Here Morrison invokes personification with the songs caressing. Add a conjunction and a dependent clause (and while she ...) that introduces one aspect of your character. Now add another independent clause (her body trembled ...) and introduce a different aspect of your character. Use series with three direct objects (redemption/salvation/rebirth).

52

Lists provide so many opportunities for style. Here is Dillard playing with the technique of epistrophe, repeating the word "it."

> *One of the few things I know about writing is this: spend it all, shoot it, play it, lose it, right away, every time.*
>
> —*The Writing Life*, Annie Dillard

Write a sentence that includes a list of at least four imperatives. Keep them short for speed. Can you add epistrophe—repeating a word or phrase at the end of each imperative?

53

How do you capture immense loss? This sentence illustrates one way.

Shuffling around, waiting for shock to give way, waiting for any kind of structured feeling to emerge from the organizational fakery of my days.

—*Grief is the Thing with Feathers,* Max Porter

Porter uses ellipsis—the deliberate omission of a word or words readily implied by context—dropping the "I" at the beginning of his sentence. The "I" has disintegrated due to the loss. If this was written in a traditional way, it would be, "I was shuffling around, waiting ..." Start a sentence without a subject. Now string together two -ing verbs, repeating one of these verbs twice, as if the subject can't move beyond this verb (waiting).

54

Parentheticals can heighten the suspense because they create delay.

> *But to go deeper, beneath what people said (and these judgements, how superficial, how fragmentary they are!) in her own mind now, what did it mean to her, this thing she called life?*
>
> —*Mrs. Dalloway*, Virginia Woolf

You'll use an interrogatory sentence. To delay the end of the sentence, add a long parenthetical. In that parenthetical, can you use anaphora (how superficial, how fragmentary)?

55

The magical power of metaphor!

His canines were obelisks.

> —*The Hero of This Book*, Elizabeth McCracken

A simple sentence but so much is accomplished. Take a body part, as McCracken did with "canines." To create humor compare it to something that is not in the human realm. The gap between the human domain and the other domain—in this case, a stone pillar—is unexpected.

56

Metaphors emerge from inhabiting a character's point of view. This sentence shows how a little boy views his father.

> *He kneeled—a mountain of shirtfront and trousers; a mountain that poured, clambered down, folded itself, re-formed itself: a disorderly massiveness, near to me, fabric-hung-and-draped: Sinai.*
>
> —"His Son, in His Arms, in Light, Aloft" by Harold Brodkey

Open with a subject and verb. Add an em dash and compare the subject to something else. This is the metaphor that will extend throughout the sentence. Add a semicolon. Now use the image from the metaphor and add four verbs. Add a colon and take a piece of that metaphor—here it's "massiveness" and a piece of the earlier version of the metaphor, "fabric-hung-and-draped." Add one more colon and introduce a final powerful image related to the metaphor.

PART FOUR

Diction

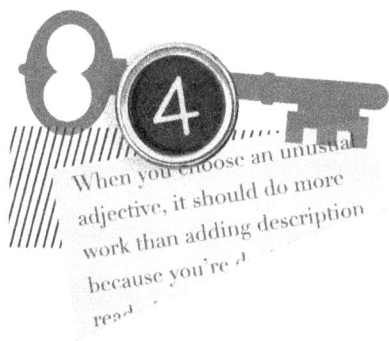

When you choose an unusual
adjective, it should do more
work than adding description
because you're d
rea

57

I hear my English teacher chiding me not to use the same word. "You have a thesaurus!" she says. Yet sometimes repetition is the best way to create meaning.

Each man is stubbornly, stubbornly himself.

—*Herzog*, Saul Bellow

Write a simple sentence—a subject and verb predicate. Use a linking verb and then repeat a word, maybe an adverb like Bellow did, to add emphasis.

58

An astonishing sentence! I could go on and on about this. Truly, Morrison is a master of style.

> *The beautiful, beautiful boys who dotted the landscape like jewels, split the air with their shouts in the field, and thickened the river with their shining wet backs.*
>
> —*Sula*, Toni Morrison

This is a mid-branching sentence with modifying information separating the subject (boys) from the verb (split). Write your subject and add an adjective—twice. Do you feel the heightened emotion that comes with repetition? Separate your subject and verb with a relative clause (who dotted) and a simile (like jewels). Now include two verbs (split/thickened). Want to do more? Go back and add assonance (split/with/thickened/river).

59

I love the surprise at the end of this sentence! What movement—from feeling free to angry.

> *She had never felt so free, so lonely so invisible or*
> *so angry.*
>
> —"Assumption" by Molly Giles

Write a simple sentence. Use four adjectives to describe your subject and also employ anaphora—the repetition of a word ("so") to create more musicality—in front of each adjective. Can the last adjective contrast with the others to create surprise?

60

So much work is accomplished with the word "sometimes." We get a sense of what usually goes on—the habitual action—the people coming and going.

> *Sometimes they came and went without having met Gatsby at all, came for the party with a simplicity of heart that was its own ticket of admission.*
>
> —*The Great Gatsby*, F. Scott Fitzgerald

Open your sentence with "Sometimes" or "Usually." Now include two verbs and use antithesis (came/went). Add one more clause that repeats one of your verbs (came).

STUNNING SENTENCES

61

I love this sentence not only for the energy of all those verbs, but the power of exposition. Workshops might make you think otherwise, but you don't need to show everything.

> *Instead of waiting for her alarm to ring, she got up, showered, dressed, drank a cup of coffee, and loaded her car.*
>
> —*Thinks,* David Lodge

Write a sentence with five verbs to create energy. Can you open with an adverbial clause that includes more verbs (waiting/ring)?

STUNNING SENTENCES

62

So much emotion in this sentence because of the proliferation of adjectives. The sentence refuses restraint and containment. It's clear the voice has a strong opinion.

> *Everything he writes is written as an angry, passionate, generous, fumbling, rebellious, bewildered and bewildering man.*
>
> —*The Vanishing Hero*, Sean O'Faolain

Write a list of adjectives—more than three! Once you stretch beyond three, there is a sense of the irrational, the emotional. Can you add polyptoton—repeating a word but in a different form (writes/written, bewildered/bewildering).

63

When I revise, one whole revision is spent on diction. Can I find a better word? One that is more specific? Or invites figurative meaning? One that fits my themes?

> *She was thinking that the palms were livid with green death.*
>
> —"Tall Tales from the Mekong Delta" by Kate Braverman

Write a right-branching sentence and choose a word (a subject complement) that either creates personification or gestures to it. Here, the palms are livid with green death. Livid means angry and also dark bluish gray in color.

64

I really like the echo of "married" in this sentence, and how at the end Lahiri finds another use for the word.

Never married, but, like all women, I've had my share of married men.

— "Casting Shadows" by Jhumpa Lahiri

Use ellipsis and eliminate your subject (I) to create a colloquial tone. Then use "but," which indicates a turn in the sentence. The sentence was starting out one way, but now heads another direction. Can the end of your sentence repeat a word from the beginning of the sentence? Can you take it one step further and use the word to create a different meaning for it?

STUNNING SENTENCES

140

65

I've read this story so many times and this opening sentence still makes me laugh.

> *By our second day at Camp Crescendo, the girls in*
> *my Brownie troop had decided to kick the asses of*
> *each and every girl in Brownie Troop 909.*
>
> —"Brownies" by ZZ Packer

In one sentence mix high register language—polysyllabic, Latinate words—and low register, more colloquial words to create range of sounds and humor. Packer juxtaposes "Crescendo" and "kick the asses" and then there's that splash of hyperbole with "each and every."

66

Here's the sentence you recite to your workshop when they demand more specificity, but you're interested in creating suspense via delay.

> *I read it, and I couldn't believe it, and I read it again.*

—"Sonny's Blues" by James Baldwin

Write three independent clauses and connect them with the conjunction "and." End each clause with the same word—this is called epistrophe. Can you use a pronoun as the repeating word (it)? For the final independent clause, break the rhythm slightly by adding one extra word (again).

67

I love the alliteration and the specificity of the adjectives!

The girl couldn't act, but she was dewy, doelike.

—*Fates and Furies,* Lauren Groff

Write two independent clauses and connect them with a conjunction. Now write two adjectives and use alliteration to describe the subject of the second independent clause. Use asyndeton—the lack of a conjunction—so the adjectives are pressed together as Groff does (dewy, doelike) to draw more attention to the alliteration.

68

With this sentence, I hear my kids talking. "Stuff" is a favorite word in our family. "I don't know, Mom, we're going to do some stuff."

> *We stayed in our PJs and people visited and gave us stuff.*
>
> —*Grief is the Thing with Feathers,* Max Porter

To create a young voice, write two short independent clauses and connect them with a conjunction. Now consider diction. Not polysyllabic words, but monosyllabic and often imprecise diction, such as "stuff."

_____

_____

_____

_____

_____

_____

69

Once I understand what my story is about, I revise, remembering this sentence and the power of diction.

> *The final dying sounds of their dress rehearsal left the Laurel Players with nothing to do but stand there, silent and helpless, blinking out over the footlights of an empty auditorium.*
>
> *Revolutionary Road,* Richard Yates

One word. A single word can color the entire sentence and convey a major thematic thread in a story. In Yates' sentence, it's "dying." Write a simple sentence, a subject and verb predicate. Think about your major themes and add an adjective that suggests this theme.

70

The colloquial voice in this sentence is terrific!

And quite naturally we laughed at her, laughed the way we did at the junk man who went about his business like he was some big-time president and his sorry-ass horse his secretary.

—"The Lesson" by Toni Cade Bambara

You can create an oral quality to your sentence by opening with a conjunction, such as "and." It also connects this sentence with the previous one. Now let your character's diction seep into the sentence via invented adjectives (some big-time, sorry-ass).

PART FIVE

Imagery

5

"For the minimalist writer, the
images, events and situation
must do double-duty, providing
the 'formula' for ?
of tʰ

71

I love the way this sentence builds to a surprising image.

> *If the world were a right place, a place for the living, a place where men like Michael didn't end up in jail, I'd be able to find wild strawberries.*
>
> —*Sing, Unburied, Sing*, Jesmyn Ward

This is a left-branching sentence. Open with "If" and use anadiplosis—end the first clause or phrase with a word (place)—and begin the next phrase with the same word (place). Add another clause that begins with that repeated word. Now end with an independent clause. Can you include an unexpected image?

72

I so clearly see the snow-removal machine because of the beautiful image.

Spraying wings of snow, a snow-removal machine, its yellow lights revolving, disappeared down Eighteenth like the last blinks of electricity.

—"Chopin in Winter" by Stuart Dybek

This is a mid-branching sentence, but first open with a present participial phrase, using an ing verb that describes your subject. Can you add personification to this image? Now write the subject of the sentence (snow-removal machine) and follow with more description of your subject (called an appositive). Now add your verb and a simile.

73

This sentence feels magical with its yellow cocktail music.

The lights grow brighter as the earth lurches away from the sun, and now the orchestra is playing yellow cocktail music, and the opera of voices pitches a key higher.

—*The Great Gatsby,* F. Scott Fitzgerald

Start with your subject/verb. Now add a subordinate clause that creates a vertical spike—something that sends the reader up above the scene (as the earth lurches ...). Next, bring the reader back to the ground and return to the original scene with two independent clauses. Can you invoke synesthesia, in which one sense triggers another sense (yellow cocktail music) with the auditory triggering the visual?

STUNNING SENTENCES

74

I have a sweet spot for personification. For me, it makes the world wondrous.

In a vision, he saw the sea rising up to suck them in, tonguing off their flesh and rolling their bones over its coral molars in the deep.

—*Fates and Furies,* Lauren Groff

A series of three creates more sound and rhythm. Write three -ing adjectives—present participles—to describe a noun, such as Groff does to depict the sea (rising, tonguing, rolling). Want personification? Use present participles that personify an inanimate noun.

75

Sentences are alive. They can help us see the world anew.

It's small and red with tight steps in front and windows so small you'd think they were holding their breath.

—*The House on Mango Street,* Sandra Cisneros

Use a right-branching sentence. The "it" in this sentence is a house, which is the subject. Use personification and animate the inanimate. Here, the windows as so small they seem to be holding their breath.

76

The simile in this sentence always makes me laugh.

> *My son slept sitting in a chair like some boozed commuter, head rolling on his chest.*
>
> —*White Noise*, Don DeLillo

Write a right-branching sentence and use a simile to describe your subject. You can invite humor by using an unusual comparison. Add one more modifying phrase at the end to help the reader see the subject.

77

I don't know why but verbs that animate the inanimate send shivers through me. Maybe it reminds me that there is so much that is still unknowable about the world.

> *Tallow candles in red glass jars shudder on a high altar.*
>
> —*Mariette in Ecstasy*, Ron Hansen

Write a simple sentence. Choose a verb that conveys a comparison, thus creating a verb metaphor. Here, candles are shuddering, which suggests they are alive, animated.

78

This pared down list lets the images dominate.

The silver of cleaned knives and metal tables, the silver of slabs of fish, of fish heads, eyes still with shock, mouths cocked open.

—"River So Close" by Melinda Moustakis

Make a list. Now try ellipsis, a technique in which a word or words are omitted from the sentence, with one effect being exhaustion. Here, the verb has dropped out. Is there an image that you want to draw the most attention to? If so, repeat it like Moustakis did with "silver" and "fish."

79

This sentence stretches and freshens language. I've never heard someone described like this. It makes me want to push language further.

He was the kind of man who walks into a room and all the walls fall down.

—*I'll Give You the Sun*, Jandy Nelson

Write a sentence that describes how your subject affects a room. Use hyperbole, such as Nelson does. How do you do this? Start with the usual description. In Nelson's sentence, one interpretation is that the character has a big presence. When he enters the room, everyone knows it. Now free associate and exaggerate.

80

This sentence feels like a build-up to the crescendo of an astonishing image.

> *The falling snow and the early hour conspired to make Prague ghostly, like a tintype photograph, all silver and haze.*
>
> —*Daughter of Smoke & Bone,* Laini Taylor

Use a compound subject for more rhythm and sound. Include assonance (falling/Prague, snow/ghostly/photograph, make/haze). Now use a simile to make your image more vivid, and finally, invoke balance and add two more adjectives

STUNNING SENTENCES

81

So much vivid detail! It's a long sentence, but the use of repetition through anaphora acts as an anchor, helping me travel through it without getting lost.

> *I see the edge of the grey tarmac and every individual blade of grass, I see the hare leaping out of its hiding-place, with its ears laid back and a curiously human expression on its face that was rigid with terror and strangely divided; and in its eyes, turning to look back as it fled and almost popping out of its head with fright, I see myself, become one with it.*

> —*Rings of Saturn*, W. G. Sebald

Write three independent clauses and use anaphora— repeating the same word or words at the beginning of each clause (I see). Connect the first two clauses with a comma, creating a comma splice. Because you're practicing, you can use the verb "see." Include three images (tarmac, grass, hare). Before you add the third independent clause, usher in modifying information. Connect it by using a semicolon.

In the final independent clause, refer to the third image mentioned in the second independent clause.

82

I love how this sentence makes me really see the smile by the accumulation of specific details.

> *But his smile was so expert—not the least bit furtive or the least bit vain, a perfectly open, friendly smile—that he could see the assurance come back into her face before he got to the desk.*
>
> —*Revolutionary Road*, Richard Yates

Make an image adhere in the reader's mind by adding precise details. Write a right-branching sentence. Now modify the subject with four adjectives. Can you add anaphora as Yates did with "the least bit"?

83

Metaphors can make such unexpected comparisons and images. I included two sentences here so you can see how the metaphor seeps into the entire passage.

> *Lynn's face, which had aged into the early years of her forties with little modification of her cool detached beauty, was architecturally designed for such outrageous confessions. Her high cheekbones kept her eyes buttressed from the collapse of a disbelieving brow, her nearly crow's feet-free eyes never gave way to an off-putting squint, and her mouth, flanked on both sides by a single parenthesis of a gently etched laugh line, remained in perfect equipoise when presented with revelations that would have provoked lesser professionals fallen jaws of slackened disgust or a steady stream of rebuke.*
>
> —*Then We Came to the End*, Joshua Ferris

Write a mid-branching sentence, separating your subject (face) from the verb (was) with a modifying phrase or clause.

Introduce a metaphor that will lead to subsequent sentences that extend the metaphor (architecturally). In Ferris's sentence he uses "buttressed" to stretch the metaphor.

84

This sentence begins a turn in this short story, and what was grounded in reality starts to become strange.

> *The moon that night was bright and full, but after a while it began to seem damaged to me, marked by some small inaccuracy.*
>
> —"The Ceiling" by Kevin Brockmeier

Use a right-branching sentence and use a familiar image as the subject. Add two adjectives that again are familiar. Add the conjunction "but" so you can set off in a new direction. Now add a second independent clause that introduces an adjective making the original image less familiar.

85

Faulkner must have felt such delight in crafting this sentence!

He flows upward in a stooping swirl like the lash of a whip, his body in midair shaped to the horse.

—*As I Lay Dying,* William Faulkner

Use a simile to compare a human to the shape of an object. Here, a character is compared to the "lash of a whip." Can you add alliteration (stooping/swirl)? Now add a modifying phrase or clause to further draw the picture.

86

The image is so strong because it's vivid and specific and original.

> *The street was witness to the fresh glowing newness in him.*
>
> —*The Heart in Winter*, Kevin Barry

A simple sentence with a linking verb. The power comes from the innovative way of describing a character who has fallen in love. Take an emotion, such as new love, and think of two adjectives and a noun that capture how that emotion has changed your character.

Glossary: Grammar

Adjective: A word that describes a noun or a pronoun.

Adverb: A word that describes a verb, an adjective, another adverb, or a sentence, expressing a relation to time, manner, place, or degree.

Adverbial phrase: A group of words that functions as an adverb.

Base clause: See <u>independent clause.</u>

Clause: A group of related words containing a subject and predicate.

Comma splice: The joining of two independent clauses with a comma rather than a conjunction or semicolon.

Complex sentence: Contains an independent clause and at least one dependent clause.

Compound sentence: Contains at least two independent clauses joined together by a coordinating conjunction or a semicolon.

Compound/complex sentence: Contains two independent clauses and at least one dependent clause.

Coordinating conjunction: A conjunction that connects words, phrases, and clauses that are coordinate, or equal to each other. There are seven coordinating conjunctions: for, and, nor, but, or, yet, so. They can be remembered using the acronym FANBOYS.

Cumulative sentence: An independent clause followed by a series of free modifying phrases or subordinate clauses. It gets its name because it accumulates information, gathering new details as it continues.

Dependent clause: A dependent clause, also known as a "subordinate clause," is a group of words that includes a subject and a verb, but it doesn't express a complete thought and cannot function as a sentence on its own.

Direct object: A noun or pronoun that receives the action of a transitive verb.

Free-modifying phrase: A modifying phrase is "free" when it can be placed at the beginning, middle or end of a sentence. The only requirement is that the placement make sense by being close enough to what it modifies so as to avoid confusion.

Fused sentence: Two independent clauses joined without any punctuation.

High register language: A level of language that is formal, precise, and more complex, often used in professional, academic, or official settings.

Imperative: A sentence that gives a command, makes a request or offers advice. It typically has an implied subject of "you."

Independent clause: Also known as the "main clause" or "base clause," it has a subject and verb and can stand alone as a complete sentence.

Indirect object: The recipient of the verb. To or for whom or what the action of the verb is performed.

Infinitive phrase: A group of words that begins with an infinitive (a verb form preceded by "to") and may include modifiers, objects, or complements.

Interrogative sentence: Asks a question, often beginning with who, what, where, when, why or how.

Left-branching sentence: The modifying information comes at the beginning of the sentence, delaying the independent clause (base clause/main clause) until the end.

Linking verb: Connects the subject of a sentence to a subject complement (an adjective, noun, or pronoun that describes or identifies the subject) rather than expressing an action.

Low register language: Informal, casual language styles often used in everyday conversations and social settings. It's characterized by the use of slang, colloquialisms, contractions, and vernacular grammar.

Mid-branching sentence: The modifying information usually comes in between the subject and the verb of the sentence, delaying the verb.

Modifying phrase: Information that modifies some aspect of the independent clause—the subject, verb, verb predicate, or the entire sentence.

Phrase: A group of two or more words that functions as a single unit within a sentence but lacks both a subject and a predicate, meaning it cannot stand alone as a complete sentence.

Present participle: A word derived from a verb and ending in –ing that can be used as an adjective or verb.

Relative clause: a dependent clause that functions like an adjective, providing more information about a noun or noun phrase, and is often introduced by a relative pronoun (like "that," "which," "who," "whom," "whose").

Relative pronoun: A pronoun that introduces a relative clause, also known as an adjective clause, which provides additional information about a noun in a sentence.

Right-branching sentence: The independent clause comes at the beginning of the sentence with modifying information placed to the right of the independent clause.

Sentence: A group of words containing a subject (also called the noun phrase) and predicate (verb phrase) that expresses a proposition.

Simple sentence: Contains a subject and a verb predicate.

Subordinate clause: A clause that cannot stand alone as a complete sentence.

Subordinate conjunction: Introduces the subordinate clause.

Subject complement: A word or phrase that follows a linking verb and either renames or describes the subject of a sentence.

Syntax: The way in which words are ordered to form phrases or clauses.

Transitive verb: A verb that requires an object (feel, address, bring, offer, have…).

Glossary: Rhetoric

Alliteration: The repetition of like consonant sounds at the beginning of words.

Anacoluthon: A grammatical interruption or lack of implied sequence within a sentence.

Analogy: A comparison of two otherwise unlike things based on resemblance of a particular aspect.

Anadiplosis: The last word(s) of a phrase or clause is repeated at the beginning of the next phrase or clause for heightened emotion and rhythmic effect.

Anaphora: The repetition of the same word(s) at the beginning of successive phrases or clauses for heightened emotion and rhythmic effect.

Anastrophe: Inversion of the usual word order.

Antithesis: The use of parallel structure—typically, but not always—to juxtapose contrasting, often seemingly contradictory ideas.

Assonance: The repetition of vowel sounds.

Asyndeton: The deliberate omission of conjunctions for speed.

Balance: The pairing of things, or the use of two, including sounds, syllables, phrases, clauses.

Colloquialism: the use of informal, everyday language in writing.

Consonance: The repetition of consonant sounds.

Diction: The use of specific word choice.

Ellipsis: The deliberate omission of a word or words readily implied by context.

Epistrophe: The repetition of the same word or group of words at the end of successive phrases or clauses.

Hard stress: A word or syllable spoken loudly.

Hyperbaton: The inversion of the usual order of words (more than one word).

Hyperbole: The use of a word or words to create a heightened effect through deliberate exaggeration. Hyperbole is often used for serious, comic, or ironic effect.

Iamb: The rhythm pattern of soft stress followed by a heavier stress.

Metaphor: An implied comparison between two unlike things that surprisingly have some property in common.

Metonymy: Invoking a part to stand for the whole by using an attribute of the whole.

Mimesis: Imitation, mimicry.

Objective correlative: T.S. Eliot used this phrase to describe "a set of objects, a situation, a chain of events which shall be the formula of that *particular* emotion."

Parallelism: The repetition of the same grammatical form in two or more parts of a sentence.

Parenthesis: The insertion of some verbal unit in a position that interrupts the normal syntactical flow of a sentence. A dash, parenthesis, or comma can be used.

Personification: Investing an inanimate object or an abstraction with human qualities.

Plosive sounds: Also called stops, these are consonants produced by completely blocking the airflow in the mouth and then releasing it suddenly, creating a "burst" or "explosion" effect. In English, there are six plosive sounds: /p/, /b/, /t/, /d/, /k/, and /g/.

Polyptoton: The repetition of words with the same root but different forms or endings.

Polysyndeton: The deliberate use of more conjunctions than is necessary.

Register: The range of diction used for different situations.

Rhythm: An ordered recurrent alternation of strong and weak elements in the flow of sound and silence in speech.

Series: The use of three things, such as sounds, syllables, words, phrases, clauses.

Simile: An explicit comparison between two unlike things, using "like" or "as."

Soft stress: A word or syllable spoken softly.

Synecdoche: A figure of speech by which a part is used to stand for the whole.

Synesthesia: A subjective sensation or image of a sense—such as color—other than the one being stimulated—such as sound.

Syntactic symbolism: Language that is arranged to look or sound like the content of the sentence.

Trope: A figure of speech, turn of phrase, or idea that carries a deeper meaning beyond its literal meaning.

Learn More about Sibyl Writing
Craft Books and Courses

About the Author

For more than twenty years, Nina Schuyler has shared her love of teaching and writing with students of all levels. Author of *How to Write Stunning Sentences*, she teaches for Stanford Continuing Studies, Book Passage, and Sibyl Writing Craft, and writes the Stunning Sentences Substack. Her classes blend play and discipline, creating welcoming spaces where writers take risks, stretch their voices, and build supportive community. Also an acclaimed novelist, her award-winning works include *In This Ravishing World* and *Afterword*, with fiction published in *Zyzzyva, Chicago Quarterly Review*, and nominated for the Pushcart Prize.

Acknowledgments

I am indebted to the many brilliant writers who came before me, most of whom you'll find in this book because they married stunning sentences with unforgettable stories that burned in my brain, turning my imagination into a wild being.

I am equally indebted to my students, who ask the best questions and make me think more deeply about the how and why of a sentence. Why write it this way? What meaning is created? Can I do this? I've had to learn how to articulate clear answers to these questions. (I hope the questions never end.) And then, after learning a new style technique, the gorgeousness and inventiveness that flows from my students' brains onto the page! How surprised they are that they can write like this! How amazing that one stunning sentence can unfold into a story. I can feel the lightning in the air and have continued teaching all these years to experience that again and again.

This manuscript owes a great deal to Brian Hurley, the former publisher of Fiction Advocate, who encouraged me to write the original version of this book. And Vicki DeArmon, publisher of Sybilline Press, who suggested I write a second edition. Thank you.

And to the sentence itself, which I've come to view as pulsing with life and sound and rhythm.

Sibylline Press is proud to publish the brilliant work of women authors over 50. We are a woman-owned publishing company and, like our authors, represent women of a certain age.

How to Write Stunning Sentences • Living the Life: Writing Vivid, Memorable Characters • The Joys and Challenges of Revision: A Hands-on Approach to Forming and Finishing a Project for Publication • A Writer's Resolution: Setting Your Goals for the New Year • The Sound of Story–Finding, Crafting and Playing with Voice • 'Tude and Tone: How Attitude and Opinion Shape Page Turning Characters • Voice and POV: Shifting Perspectives, Shifting Voice • When the Character is You: Curating Voice in the Memoir or Essay • Voice Up Your Non-Fiction: How to Capture and Keep Reader Attention • Tone, Emotion and Mood: Controlling Your Readers' Feelings • The Sound of Story–Finding Crafting and Playing with Voice • Lyrical Writing For Plot-Forward Writers • Revising for Voice: Polishing This Key Element of Successful Writing • Experiments in Voice: Breaking Free From Usual Forms • Sound of Story: Voice and Tone Immersion • Looking to the Past: How to Research your Historical Fiction • Writing from Multiple Viewpoints • The Tough Love Publishing Intensive: Get Real. Get Ready. Get Published • Path to Publication • Are You Actually Ready to Publish? • Ask Us Anything — Live Publishing Strategy Q&A • One Book Won't Pay the Bills: Real Talk About Author Income, Career Growth, and Making It Work • Social Media for Authors: The Good, the Bad, and the Absolutely Necessary • Pitch Perfect: Sell Your Book to Bookstores, Libraries, and Gatekeepers • Understanding Rights and Licensing • Understanding the World of Book Publishing • Acquisitions for Noobs: How to get through the door! • On the Frontlines with Bookstores • Bookstore Presentation Coaching by an Expert

Learn more about our books and courses!

Books and Courses Designed for Writers

Sibylline Press is thrilled to introduce our new writing craft series paired with online writing courses.

Sibyl Writing Craft's 2026 courses include 30 different offerings taught by our instructors, each dedicated to different aspects of writing and the business of book publishing. Our instructors (we call them mentors) are women of a certain age with years of wisdom and experience and they include many of our partners at Sibylline Press. And yes, we are all writers as well.

Each year, as writers, we think about what we will accomplish in the coming year. We set our goals and revisit our ambitions. It may be to improve some aspect of our craft, to hone the work we have, to start something new, to achieve publication, or to jumpstart our author skills once published.

At Sibyl Writing Craft, we can revel with you at the sentence level or help you polish your manuscripts using the tools of voice, tone, character, and point of view, to name a few. We can assist with your revisions. We can walk you through the book industry and how it really works. We can shed light on how licensing and rights work or train you on social media. We can provide a road map for indie authors to capitalize on every opportunity. We can train you to present to bookstores. We know you will delight in our range offerings as much as we delighted in creating them.

Our courses are designed as Confabs, which are 75-minute informational talks on a topic, and the longer Labs, which provide more interactivity for participants on a given subject over three or more sessions. Each Confab or Lab comes with one of our Sibyl Writing Craft books on that subject and is taught by that author. Most Confabs and Labs take place on Zoom. Some take place in partner bookstores.

In addition to offering fabulous courses, we've got gifts. Upon enrollment in our Confabs or Labs this first year, you'll receive a complimentary copy of *A Writer's Resolution*. This writer's journal will help you plan your writing future.

We can't wait to collaborate with you on your writing and publishing journey. We are invested in your success as a writer. And as a book publisher, the team at Sibylline Press even hopes to see your best work in our submissions portal.

To learn more about our Confabs or Labs for the year, please see our catalog at sibyllinepress.com

Titles Coming in 2026

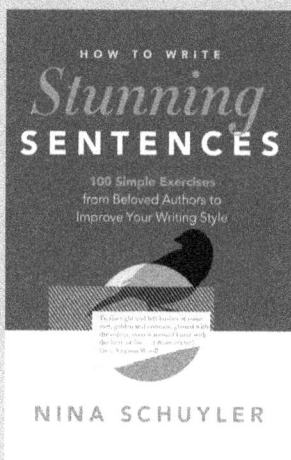

HOW TO WRITE
Stunning
SENTENCES

100 Simple Exercises
from Beloved Authors to
Improve Your Writing Style

NINA SCHUYLER

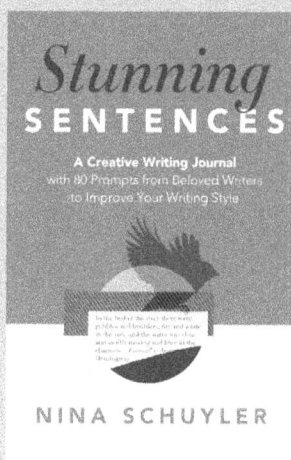

Stunning
SENTENCES

A Creative Writing Journal
with 80 Prompts from Beloved Writers
to Improve Your Writing Style

NINA SCHUYLER

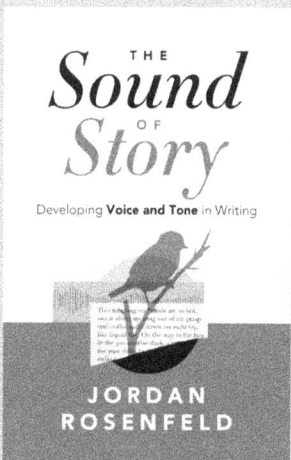

THE
Sound
OF
Story

Developing **Voice and Tone** in Writing

JORDAN
ROSENFELD

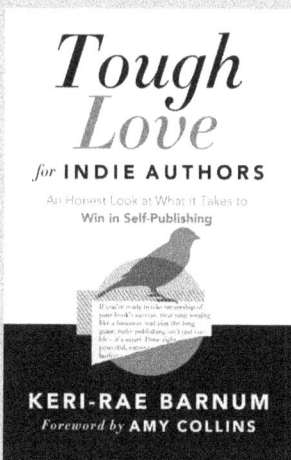

Tough
Love
for **INDIE AUTHORS**

An Honest Look at What it Takes to
Win in Self-Publishing

KERI-RAE BARNUM
Foreword by **AMY COLLINS**

PLUS: *A Writer's Resolution: A Guided Journal for Realizing a Rewarding Writing Practice* By Christine Walker